BASKETBALL LEGENDS

Kareem Abdul-Jabbar
Charles Barkley
Larry Bird
Kobe Bryant
Wilt Chamberlain
Clyde Drexler
Julius Erving
Patrick Ewing
Kevin Garnett
Anfernee Hardaway
Tim Hardaway
The Head Coaches
Grant Hill
Juwan Howard
Allen Iverson
Magic Johnson
Michael Jordan
Shawn Kemp
Jason Kidd
Reggie Miller
Alonzo Mourning
Hakeem Olajuwon
Shaquille O'Neal
Gary Payton
Scottie Pippen
David Robinson
Dennis Rodman
John Stockton
Keith Van Horn
Antoine Walker
Chris Webber

CHELSEA HOUSE PUBLISHERS

BASKETBALL LEGENDS

CHRIS WEBBER

Paul J. Deegan

Introduction by
Chuck Daly

CHELSEA HOUSE PUBLISHERS
Philadelphia

Produced by Combined Publishing, Inc.

CHELSEA HOUSE PUBLISHERS

Editor in Chief: Stephen Reginald
Managing Editor: James Gallagher
Production Manager: Pamela Loos
Art Director: Sara Davis
Director of Photography: Judy L. Hasday
Senior Production Editor: Lisa Chippendale
Publishing Coordinator: James McAvoy
Cover Design and Digital Illustration: Keith Trego

Cover Photos: AP/Wide World Photos

The Chelsea House World Wide Web site address is
http://www.chelseahouse.com

First Printing

1 3 5 7 9 8 6 4 2

Library of Congress Cataloging-in-Publication Data

Deegan, Paul J., 1937-
    Chris Webber / Paul J. Deegan.
       p.   cm. — (Basketball legends)
    Includes bibliographical references (p.) and index.
    Summary: A biography of the young player who was a member of the
University of Michigan's "Fab Five" in 1993 and Rookie of the Year
in the NBA the next year.
    ISBN   0-7910-5010-6
    1. Webber, Chris, 1973-   —Juvenile literature.   2. Basketball
players—United States—Biography—Juvenile literature.
[1. Webber, Chris, 1973-   . 2. Basketball players.   3. Afro-
Americans—Biography.]   I. Title.   II. Series.
GV884.W36D44   1988
796.232'092—dc21
[B]   98-31350
                                                   CIP
                                                         AC

CONTENTS

BECOMING A BASKETBALL LEGEND   6
CHUCK DALY

CHAPTER 1
EVERY OUNCE OF HIS SOUL   9

CHAPTER 2
A MAN AMONG BOYS   15

CHAPTER 3
THE PATH TO ANN ARBOR   23

CHAPTER 4
THE FRESHMAN ASSEMBLE   31

CHAPTER 5
THE "FAB FIVE" AND THE FINAL FOUR
39

CHAPTER 6
ON TO THE NBA   47

CHAPTER 7
"REMARKABLE EFFORT"
FALLS SHORT   53

CHRONOLOGY   60
STATISTICS   61
FURTHER READING   62
INDEX   64

BECOMING A BASKETBALL LEGEND

Chuck Daly

What does it take to be a basketball superstar? Two of the three things it takes are easy to spot. Any great athlete must have excellent skills and tremendous dedication. The third quality needed is much harder to define, or even put in words. Others call it leadership or desire to win, but I'm not sure that explains it fully. This third quality relates to the athlete's thinking process, a certain mentality and work ethic. One can coach athletic skills, and while few superstars need outside influence to help keep them dedicated, it is possible for a coach to offer some well-timed words in order to keep that athlete fully motivated. But a coach can do no more than appeal to a player's will to win; how much that player is then capable of ensuring victory is up to his own internal workings.

In recent times, we have been fortunate to have seen some of the best to play the game. Larry Bird, Magic Johnson, and Michael Jordan had all three components of superstardom in full measure. They brought their teams to numerous championships, and made the players around them better. (They also made their coaches look smart.)

I myself coached a player who belongs in that class, Isiah Thomas, who helped lead the Detroit Pistons to consecutive NBA crowns. Isiah is not tall—he's just over six feet—but he could do whatever he wanted with the ball. And what he wanted to do most was lead and win.

All the players I mentioned above and those whom this series will chronicle are tremendously gifted athletes, but for the most part, you can't play professional basketball at all unless you have excellent skills. And few players get to stay on their team unless they are willing to dedicate themselves to improving their talents even more, learning about their opponents, and finding a way to join with their teammates and win.

It's that third element that separates the good player from the superstar, the memorable players from the legends of the game. Superstars know when to take over the game. If the situation calls for a defensive stop, the superstars stand up and do it. If the situation calls for a key pass, they make it. And if the situation calls for a big shot, they want the ball. They don't want the ball simply because of their own glory or ego. Instead they know—and their teammates know—that they are the ones who can deliver, regardless of the pressure.

The words "legend" and "superstar" are often tossed around without real meaning. Taking a hard look at some of those who truly can be classified as "legends" can provide insight into the things that brought them to that level. All of them developed their legacy over numerous seasons of play, even if certain games will always stand out in the memories of those who saw them. Those games typically featured amazing feats of all-around play. No matter how great the fans thought the superstars were, these players were capable of surprising the fans, their opponents, and occasionally even themselves. The desire to win took over, and with their dedication and athletic skills already in place, they were capable of the most astonishing achievements.

CHUCK DALY, now the head coach of the Orlando Magic, guided the Detroit Pistons to two straight NBA championships, in 1989 and 1990. He earned a gold medal as coach of the 1992 U.S. Olympic basketball team—the so-called "Dream Team"—and was inducted into the Pro Basketball Hall of Fame in 1994.

EVERY OUNCE OF HIS SOUL

Chris Webber threw the sweat-soaked towel onto a bench. He and the other members of the Washington Bullets were frustrated as they entered the locker room after the first half of the final regular-season game of the 1996-97 season.

It was the most important game Webber had played since he and Bullets teammate Juwan Howard were stars at the University of Michigan. The winner—either Washington or the Cleveland Cavaliers—would advance to the National Basketball Association playoffs. The season would be over for the losers.

When he came on the court for the tipoff, there had been a look of fierce determination on Webber's face. But at the half, the Bullets were behind by nine.

The 1996-97 season had been Webber's best as a pro. But it was also a year when the Bullets chased the Cavaliers and almost everyone

Chris Webber grabs a rebound while Cleveland Cavalier Dan Majerle looks on.

CHRIS WEBBER

Bullets coach Bernie Bick-erstaff talks with Chris Webber and Juwan Howard during a time-out.

else in the NBA's Eastern Conference for a play-off spot. In midseason, they had been 10th among the 15 Eastern Conference teams. By February, they were five and a half games out of the eighth and final playoff position.

Now, two months later, the Bullets' entire season hung in the balance with two quarters left to play on a Sunday afternoon in Cleveland. Webber, a 6'10", 245-pound power forward, decided he wasn't going to let his team lose.

The Bullets had scored only 35 points in the first half. The home team was milking almost

every possession on offense, using up most of the 24-second clock each time, resulting in a slow-motion contest. The Cavaliers were also playing tough on defense, shutting down Howard for most of the game. The good news for the Bullets was that they trailed by only nine points at the half.

In the locker room, Bullets coach Bernie Bickerstaff told his team to sit down; he wanted them to relax. He felt they put in a poor first-half performance because they were too nervous. Point guard Rod Strickland, usually reliable, was a step too slow and had turned over the basketball three times in the game's first five minutes. Bickerstaff told his players to stay calm when they took the floor for the second half.

Webber, too, believed he had brought too much energy to the game. Now, he and his teammates had 24 minutes remaining to earn the team's first postseason berth in nine years.

It is nearly a cliché in sports that great players step up to the challenge in key situations. It turned out to be a reality that day as Webber became the star of the game. It was probably his most impressive performance of the season, in the most important game of the season.

In the first quarter, Webber scored 11 of his team's 23 points. He was all over the floor, making big plays throughout the game. But, after scoring a dismal 12 points in the second quarter, the Bullets fell behind by 11 early in the third quarter. They rallied to trail by only two entering the fourth quarter. An 11-4 run gave them a five-point lead. But it would be a pressure-packed finish with the game still in doubt going into the final minutes.

Suddenly, Webber whacked the ball away from

Chris Webber reaches over the head of an opposing teammate to give his all for a Bullets win.

a Cavalier, and the ball was loose on the floor. Though it had been a physical game and Webber was very tired, he threw his body at the ball, determined to get it. His hustle resulted in another possession, producing points for the Bullets.

With 13.3 seconds left to play, Howard, who had missed eight of his first 10 shots, buried an off-balance jumper giving Washington an 84-80 lead and sewing up a comeback 85-81 victory. The Washington Bullets were in the NBA playoffs for the first time since 1988.

During the season, Webber said the Bullets "don't just want to be a talented team. We want to be in the top four or five in the league." They weren't at that level, but thanks to Webber's big-game performance they had ended years of futility.

Webber had finished the game with 23 points and 17 rebounds, a slightly better record than the team-high 20.1 points he averaged while playing in 72 of 82 games during the season. He also led the Bullets in rebounding despite the presence of Gheorghe Muresan, the 7'7" center from Romania. Webber had 743 rebounds for a 10.3 per game average. His 137 blocked shots were also a team high. Muresan was second with 41 fewer blocks.

Saving his best for last, Webber played the 82nd and final regular season game ". . . like a man who would give every ounce of his soul just to be able to keep playing when the day came to an end," wrote columnist Jennifer Frey.

At the end of the game with Cleveland, Webber and Howard, close friends and longtime teammates, grabbed each other at midcourt. Tears were streaming down Webber's face as he hugged Howard. The tears showed how important it was to him that the team made the playoffs. All year the Bullets had been labeled an underachieving team. They cast off the label that night.

"The first few years here were so hard that to be in the playoffs is huge," Webber said.

2

A MAN AMONG BOYS

Everyone who has watched Chris Webber play basketball during the past decade agrees that he is a marvelously gifted player. He combines the strength of a big man with the agility of a backcourt player. Webber's intensity on the basketball floor also is unquestioned.

His full name is Mayce Edward Christopher Webber III, and he was born March 1, 1973, in Detroit, Michigan. He is the oldest of Mayce and Doris Webber's five children.

Chris grew up in northwest Detroit in a simple brick house on a street full of similar houses. His father was a stock keeper at a General Motors plant in Livonia. His mother was a special education teacher in the Detroit public schools. His mother, Webber said, "couldn't care less about basketball." She just wanted him to get a good education.

But for most of his life, Webber has been identified by his basketball talent even though he

Chris Webber shoots the ball for Country Day High School, already showing the skills that would take him to the NBA.

was a good student, personable, and polite. Webber's skill on the court became apparent even before he entered high school. By the time he was 13 and in the eighth grade, he was 6'5" tall. He was averaging 30 points a game for his Inkster Temple Christian team.

The college recruiting process usually begins sometime in the high school years, but colleges were already calling Chris Webber. It began at the end of his seventh grade year, when he received a letter from the Michigan State University basketball coach, Jeff Heathcote.

Chris also was being recruited for high school basketball. He dominated boys his age on the basketball court, but he was also a fine student who had a good personality and was well-mannered, making him a desirable addition to any high school's student body. The rules of the Michigan High School Athletic Association did not allow high schools to recruit, but some of the best athletes wound up attending a small list of high schools, usually private ones.

Although Chris lived in the Redford High School district, he wanted to go to Southwestern, a public high school in Detroit. He and his family were also considering several private high schools.

More than 20 high schools contacted the Webbers. Staying at Inkster Temple Christian, where he had been for two years, was also a possibility. He liked the school, which had fewer than 500 students in grades one through 12, and he had many friends there. "I might just stay here," he said. "I put God first, then my family, then basketball. I figure if I'm good enough, I'll be seen here just like I'd be if I went to a big school."

Mayce and Doris Webber wanted Chris to

Webber was sought after by college teams while he was still in the lower grades because of his innate basketball skills.

receive an education in the classroom as well as on the basketball floor. "The main thing we want for Chris is to get an education," Mayce said. "Things like basketball can be lost at any time. Wherever he goes, we want Chris to get an education."

Later, Webber said he felt "pressured all the

time. All of the people wanting me to go to their school left me a little confused."

The choices were narrowed to Inkster Temple Christian, Country Day, and Southwestern. In May 1997, Webber decided not to follow friends from the city to Southwestern and enrolled at Country Day, which had a history of fielding good athletic teams. "I selected Country Day because it was better in academics," he said. "That had to be the most important thing. Basketball can take me a long way, but I need to get the best education possible if I get hurt or something."

In July 1987, Webber played his first game with his new teammates in a summer basketball league. The team had lost its first five games in the league, but with a few dunks from the new kid they won the game 61-48.

"He certainly makes a difference, doesn't he," said Country Day coach Kurt Keener. "We're obviously pleased to have a player of his ability. We're definitely a better team with Chris."

Webber was awarded a scholarship to Country Day School, where tuition was very expensive. Scholarships based on academic merit or financial need did not violate the high school association's rules. Chris's scholarship covered the cost of much of his tuition.

When school began in the fall, Chris wore a coat and tie to school like the other boys at Country Day, which was primarily a white, upper middle-class school. It was a hard adjustment for Chris at first because he was a city kid in the suburbs, and he stood out and sometimes felt alone.

"A lot of my classmates had these stereotypes about blacks from Detroit," Webber said. "They thought we all had big gold chains, that my mom worked in a laundromat, that all my friends were thugs, that I wouldn't get good grades."

A *Detroit Free Press* reporter said Webber's personality won over his Country Day classmates. At 17, Webber was "friendly, funny, and complimentary" when he was relaxed, wrote Mitch Albom in February 1991.

Even so, Webber never felt at home at Country Day. His closest friends were black teammates from his Detroit neighborhood whose parents also had made them go to the private school.

On the basketball floor, however, Webber was right at home. By the middle of his freshman season, he was averaging more than 20 points a game.

The 1987-88 season ended for Webber's Yellowjackets when they lost in a Class C regional tournament game. Country Day was 19-4 and ranked No. 4 going into the game. But No. 2 Detroit St. Martin de Porres won 58-55.

In January of Webber's sophomore season, Country Day was ranked No. 1 in Class C. Facing unbeaten Monroe St. Mary Catholic Central, a Class B team, the Yellowjackets won 91-55. Webber headed his team toward the 1989 Michigan Class C state championship.

The top-ranked Yellowjackets shelled the Deckerville Eagles 75-37 in a state quarterfinal contest. That meant Country Day would play a semifinal game against Cassopolis, considered their toughest opponent in the tournament. Webber's reverse slam dunk in the third quarter highlighted a 75-53 thrashing of Cassopolis.

Like any young boy who loves basketball, the young Chris Webber idolized Michael Jordan. Here Webber, as a Washington Bullet, guards the legendary player.

The following night, 13,609 fans came to Chrysler Arena to watch Country Day play Ishpeming for the Class C championship. Webber took a hard fall after blocking a shot in the second quarter and sat out more than a quarter of the game. But it didn't matter as the Yellowjackets crushed their opponent, 82-43, a surprising upset because Ishpeming had lost only one game all year. Webber scored 17 points in the first half and had 25 for the game along with 16 rebounds and four blocked shots.

A few days later Webber was the only sophomore named to the five-member *Detroit Free Press* All-Metro basketball team.

When the 1989-90 basketball season began,

Webber's abilities on the court would eventually lead him to such honors as NBA Rookie of the Year.

the Yellowjackets had moved up to Class B competition. Webber, now a 6'9" junior, was a man among boys on the basketball court. Country Day had other good players, Coach Keener noted, but Webber dominated on the floor. "Chris Webber's talent doesn't end with shot-blocking, rebounding, and inside scoring," said the *Detroit Free Press.*

Trying to win another state championship in Webber's junior year, Country Day faced Grand Rapids Northview in a semifinal game before a crowd of more than 7,000 at Crisler Arena. Webber had a game-high 25 points, 15 rebounds, and three blocked shots to lead the Yellowjackets to a 70-50 victory.

The Class B championship game was March 24, 1990, at the Palace of Auburn Hills in suburban Detroit. Webber had 30 points, 14 rebounds, and eight blocked shots in a 59-54 win over Saginaw Buena Vista. Country Day became the first Michigan high school to voluntarily move up a class and win a state title in the same season. At the end of March, Webber again was named to the *Detroit Free Press* All-Metro team.

As he had from late fall into spring, Webber played basketball through the summer. Once, he figured he played about 200 games a year. In July 1990, Webber scored 30 points as his AAU team, Superfriends, beat Indiana 70-65 in the opening game of the AAU under-17 national tournament.

Webber was getting ready for his senior year season and what lay beyond.

3

THE PATH
TO ANN ARBOR

As Webber approached his final year of high school, it was clear the high school superstar was going to be one of the nation's most highly recruited high school seniors. Webber scored 38 points in one high school game—even though he sat out the fourth quarter. In another game, an alley-oop pass was too high for him to catch. He hung in the air until the ball hit the backboard, then he caught and stuffed it. Country Day coach Keener said Webber played basketball "as if God built him to do it."

Webber has very long arms—he measures 87 inches from fingertip to fingertip with his arms extended. This enhances his ability to swoop and dunk. But, as a Detroit reporter noted, "He can pass like a point guard. His body, long and thick, can find the ball through any crowd of defenders, two, three, four, they can't stop him. Watching him play, even against the better teams, is like watching a man among boys.

Webber's ability and toughness on the court led to his being recruited by many college teams—he chose Michigan.

"He towers over most of the other players and is so superior in shooting and rebounding that he frequently gets bored and tries to make fancy passes or bring the ball upcourt just to stay interested," the reporter continued. The high school senior appeared to be ". . . like a NBA player-in-training."

Webber also "talked trash" on the court. Well-mannered away from the gym, ". . . Webber, on the court, is not to be taken lightly," reporter Mitch Albom said. "He likes to dig at his opponents, mumbling, 'Don't even think about coming in here. . . . Don't even try to shoot that ball.' . . ."

Webber's ability and toughness on the court were the reasons why college coaches wanted him in their programs. The big question now was which college would it be? Just before his senior season at Country Day began, a newspaper story said Webber had eliminated the University of Michigan from his list of colleges. "I don't know where they get stuff like that," Webber said. "Michigan is still on my list of schools."

Webber had previously eliminated Indiana from his list after he made an unofficial visit to Bloomington. He went to see a friend and they were invited to watch an Indiana practice. The Hoosiers legendary coach Bobby Knight let Webber know he was interested in having him at Indiana.

Several years later, a reporter asked Webber if he ever thought of going to Indiana. "No," he said. "It's not my style of play." Knight's teams feature controlled offense focused on screening and ball movement.

What had he thought of Knight? "I thought he was nice. He ran a good practice."

A few days after the back-and-forth about Webber deciding against Michigan, the Wolverines got a verbal commitment from Chicago Vocational High School prep star Juwan Howard, a 6'9" center. The first of the players who were to become known as the "Fab Five" was in place. On November 8, the Michigan basketball team came to Country Day to hold an intrasquad scrimmage. Webber, of course, was on hand. A few days later, Howard and Jimmy King, a 6'5" guard from East High School in Plano, Texas, signed letters of intent to Michigan.

Webber had not committed to a school, and it was going to be a senior season under pressure. He removed the phone from his bedroom because it was always ringing. Along with the phone calls, he was getting up to 50 letters a week from people who wanted to recruit him. In the beginning, he read every letter he received. Now he was throwing them into a box, unopened. Four of his friends gave him keys to their homes so he could go there to get away from all the attention. Everyone wanted to know where he was going to college.

But the pressure didn't hamper his performance on the basketball floor. In January 1991, Country Day was ranked No. 1 in Class B and was playing Ypsilanti High School, No. 1 in Class A. With the Yellowjackets down by two, Webber, now 6'10" tall, dunked with six seconds to play to force overtime. He scored four of Country Day's six overtime points to reach 31 for the game in a 78-76 victory.

By late February 1991, Webber had cut his list of possible colleges to five—Michigan, Michigan State, and Minnesota of the Big Ten Conference, national powerhouse Duke in Durham,

CHRIS WEBBER

Webber's decision was a difficult one but he finally decided he'd be dunking the ball for the Michigan Wolverines.

North Carolina, and hometown Detroit Mercy. Published reports said he had made a decision and was waiting until Country Day's season finished to announce it.

In March, Webber was named Michigan's Mr. Basketball. "Every high school basketball fan in the state knew who this year's Mr. Basketball would be except Chris Webber," said the *Detroit Free Press.* Webber said the award was an honor, but "I know nothing is ever a lock."

Again it was state tournament time. The Yellowjackets were being called "the Webberville Express" and were expected to roll to a third-straight state title. However, in a state quarterfinal game, the express nearly came to a grinding halt in a close-fought game. Country Day emerged with a 66-57 win over Dearborn Divine Child in the Class B contest.

The next day, Webber went to a Detroit hotel to accept the sixth annual Gatorade Circle of Champions award as the best high school player in the nation.

On March 23, playing on a tender ankle, Webber scored 27 points and pulled down 22 rebounds as Country Day defended their Class B state title. The victory over the Bridgeport Bearcats at the Palace of Auburn Hills meant Webber had played on three straight state championship teams.

Later that day at a Detroit restaurant crowded with the news media, Webber's mother opened a plastic bag she was holding behind her back. Inside the bag was a yellow and blue baseball cap. The University of Michigan cap answered the question Chris had been asked for years. He was going to Michigan. He pulled the cap out of the bag and said, "Next year, I'm going to be a Wolverine."

It was a bittersweet moment for Doris Webber. She wanted to maintain her composure. But she couldn't when Chris began reciting verses of a church hymn. It was one that he sometimes listened to when the recruiting pressures got him down.

"Lord, I'm available to you. My will I give to you. I'll do what you will me to do. Use me Lord to show someone the way. And enable me to say: My storage is empty and I'm available to you."

For Doris Webber, it was a dream come true.

Her son's reasons for going to college in nearby Ann Arbor included his younger brothers and sister at home. He could continue to watch them grow up while he was at Michigan.

The same day Webber made his announcement, Southwestern High School's Jalen Rose committed to Michigan. What was hailed as the nation's most outstanding recruiting class was in place, after Rose and the Prospectors had won a second straight state Class A championship, 77-63, over Detroit PSL rival Northern behind Rose's 25 points.

The other recruit who would be a member of the "Fab Five" was 6'6" forward Ray Jackson from Lyndon B. Johnson High School in Austin, Texas.

Meanwhile, Webber's senior season was capped when he was named National High School Player of the Year.

Shortly after their high school seasons ended, Webber and Rose were in Springfield, Massachusetts, along with 18 other top prep players for the 14th annual McDonald's All-American Game. Both went on to play in another All-Star game, the Dapper Dan Roundball Classic in Pittsburgh.

In June, there were more All-Star games. Webber played against Rose in the Michigan All-Star festival in Battle Creek, and they were back together when a Michigan All-Star team played a similar team from Ohio in Grand Rapids.

The following month, Webber, Rose, Howard, and Voshon Lenard, a Detroit Southwestern High School All-State player who was to become a topflight player at the University of Minnesota, played on a Michigan AAU team in the 19-and-under national tournament in Jacksonville, Florida. Webber scored 31 points and had 15 rebounds in a 116-112 win over Indiana in the championship game. His teammate-to-be at Michigan, Howard, had 22 points in the game.

Also in July, Webber, playing for the Detroit Superfriends, an AAU team, had 38 points and 27 rebounds in a 121-115 win over the Arkansas Wings, and 33 points in a 102-89 victory over the Boston Amateur Basketball Club at the AAU Junior Olympics in Tallahassee, Florida.

The recruiting of the "Fab Five" by Ann Arbor continued to play out among Michigan high-school stars. In August, Dugan Fife, a standout guard on a good Clarkston High School team, made a verbal commitment to Michigan before the start of his senior year. He knew about the great recruits headed to Michigan a year ahead of him.

"They didn't get a point guard," he said. Jalen Rose was making the transition from playing small forward in high school to point guard at Michigan.

Knowing he would be part of an outstanding team, Webber was looking forward to playing for Michigan.

4

THE FRESHMEN ASSEMBLE

In mid-October, the Michigan basketball team held its first practice. Even though only two starters returned from the 1990-91 team, which went 14-15, the Wolverines were rated No. 20 in the country on the strength of their newcomers, according to the Associated Press's pre-season poll.

There were high expectations for the teenagers Michigan coach Steve Fisher had brought to the Ann Arbor campus. Webber, Juwan Howard, Jalen Rose, and Jimmy King, the prized recruits, were joined by Ray Jackson. Some said the Michigan recruiting class was the best ever in college basketball.

The freshmen's first college competition came when Michigan played its first exhibition game of the season at Crisler Arena on November 14. Only one of the freshmen—Howard—was in the starting lineup, with Rose coming off the bench to score 15 points in a 84-63 win.

Two of the "Fab Five" celebrate a win that helped take them to the NCAA Final Four, Chris Webber (4), and Jimmy King (24).

On December 2, the Wolverines played Detroit Mercy at Cobo Arena in their season opener. Webber would be starting. Just before tipoff, Webber went up to Rose and said, "This is what we've been waiting for."

Michigan won Webber's first regular-season college game, 100-74. He played 25 minutes and went seven for 10 from the field, scoring 19

Webber's long reach blocks the shot of North Carolina's Eric Montross.

points. He had a game-high 17 rebounds, but also had seven turnovers and fouled out of the game.

"I admit I need to concentrate every minute and work on my defensive schemes," he said later. "Admitting that, I know I'll be better next time."

Webber's basketball team was answering most challenges on the court. They were 14-5 by early February and ranked 15th in the country. On February 9, the Wolverines were in South Bend, Indiana, to play a 6-11 Notre Dame team in a Sunday afternoon game. There was a sellout crowd at the Athletic and Convocation Center and a national television audience was watching.

Junior guard Mike Talley, who had started for two years, did not make the trip after missing a practice. Just minutes before the game in South Bend, Coach Fisher was going over matchups in the locker room. The five freshmen were going to start a game for the first time. Webber, Howard, and Rose had been starting for a while, and King had started a game the previous week. Jackson was now number five.

"That's what we talked about from the beginning," said guard Jimmy King. "This was not something that was given to us. We've worked hard to earn these positions."

The freshmen moved out to a 14-5 lead and with King shutting down Notre Dame's leading scorer for a half, the Wolverines led by as many as 18 points. "It was a big lift," said Webber. "It was a challenge."

He responded to the challenge. Hustling at both ends of the court, he ignited the Wolverines offense. He'd get the ball inside, look for Howard, then pass to his teammate, or put it up himself. Webber scored 13 first-half points for the 15th-ranked Wolverines. "Webber is awesome," said Notre Dame coach John MacLeod. "He's the kind of guy that looks like he can go for 40 minutes and just play the game himself."

A Notre Dame rally reduced the lead to 54-50 with 6:28 to play, but Michigan held on for a 74-65 victory, the first for the "Fab Five" as starters.

"Coach went out on a limb," Webber said. "I'm sure a lot of people thought he was crazy. We wanted to show everybody he made the right decision."

The freshmen scored all of Michigan's points—Rose had 20, King celebrated his 19th birthday that day with 19, Webber finished with 17, Howard had 14, and Ray Jackson had four.

Jackson's four points says something about the move from high school stardom to big-time college basketball. As a high school star in Texas, the 6'6" Jackson had averaged 23 points a game.

As Webber put it later in the season, "In high school, I was always the No. 1 option. There were players . . . who weren't that good, and then there was me. But everyone is good [in college basketball], they could all be a No. 1 option. I don't feel as dominant as I used to. But that's why I came [to Michigan]. I'm just part of the picture."

By March, the Wolverines were 18-7 but had dropped to an 18th ranking nationally. All seven losses were in the Big Ten to go along with eight conference victories. The Big Ten season was nearing completion when Michigan faced Indiana. The Hoosiers were No. 2 in the country with a 22-4 record and were in first place in the Big Ten at 13-2.

Michigan recorded a 68-60 upset that cost Indiana a Big Ten championship. From there the Wolverines would not lose another game until they faced Duke in the NCCA championship game in early April. Webber became the first freshman ever to lead the Big Ten in rebounding, averaging 9.8 rebounds a game.

The "Fab Five" never made it a secret that they wanted to be the best team in college basketball. Their motto was "Shock the world!" They were getting a chance to do just that when they received an at-large bid to the 1992 NCAA tournament.

The Wolverines were the sixth seed in the Southeast Region. Their first tournament action was a 73-66 win over Temple in Atlanta on March

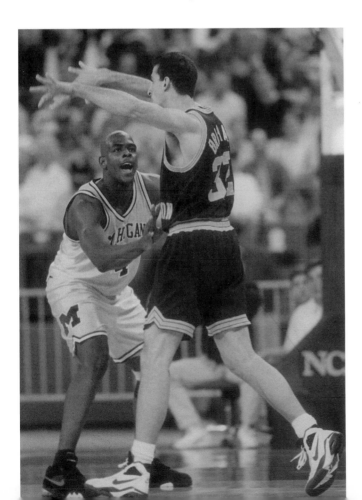

Chris Webber guards George Washington's Bill Brigham in an NCAA regional semifinal game.

20. Two days later, they beat East Tennessee State, 102-90, to advance to the regional semifinals. On March 27, in Rupp Arena on the University of Kentucky campus in Lexington, Michigan edged Oklahoma State, 75-72. In the regional finals on March 29, they faced Big-Ten rival Ohio State and got an overtime win, 75-71. The youngsters from Ann Arbor were going to the NCAA Final Four. So was Big Ten rival Indiana.

The Michigan team did not lack confidence. At a press conference during the tournament, the five freshmen sat a table before the media. Someone asked them if they really believed they could win not one, but four national championships. Their answer was yes.

A Detroit sportswriter who covered Michigan basketball said, "Such an unusual collection of basketball talent has never expected anything less. If there is one thing Webber, Rose, Howard, King, and Jackson have sought—from the time they became teammates, through the time they gang-tackled their first Crisler Arena pickup game, through the indoctrination of a roller-coaster Big Ten season . . . it is a national championship."

Greg Stoda wrote: "Good things, these kids say, do not come to those who wait. Good things, they say with a scowl, come to those who take."

Michigan's semifinal opponent in Minneapolis, Minnesota, on April 4 would be the Cincinnati Bearcats. Indiana would play the defending NCAA champions, the Duke Blue Devils.

Michigan topped Cincinnati by four points, 76-72, and Duke beat Indiana, 81-76, to set the stage for the national championship game on April 6.

Playing for a championship was not new to the Michigan players. Webber had been on three state championship teams at Country Day. So had Talley, a 1989 All-Metro teammate of Webber's whose Detroit Cooley High School team won three straight Class A championships. Rose's teams had won two state championships at Detroit Southwestern. But playing for the NCAA title was a much bigger deal.

Duke coach Mike Krzyzewski's starting five included All-America senior center Christian Laettner, sophomore forward Grant Hill, and junior guard Bobby Hurley. This was a talented and experienced unit. They were defending the NCAA championship they had won in 1991.

Hill slashed to the basket against Michigan, and Laettner scored 19 points as Duke won easily, 71-51, in a successful defense of their national title. The Blue Devils were 34-2 on the season and also ranked No. 1 in the AP poll.

Webber and Rose were named to the Final Four All-Tournament team along with the three Duke stars.

It was a near sleepless night for the young Wolverines after the loss. It was a night of talking and then a flight back to Ann Arbor the next day. There they could regroup for the 1992-93 season. But no longer would they sneak up on anyone.

They also had to deal with the talk heard during the NCAA tournament about who would be the first of the "Fab Five" to leave college and go to the NBA. Was Webber good enough to leave school early and join the NBA at age 19? The "Fab Five" had major decisions to make going into their sophomore year.

Duke's Christian Laettner battles Michigan's Webber in a 1992 NCAA Final Four game.

5

THE "FAB FIVE" AND THE FINAL FOUR

As the 1992-1993 college season approached, the question again came up: How long would Webber stay at Michigan?

The "Fab Five's" self-assured belief they would win four national championships was already history. It was increasingly unlikely they would stay together for even three years. Their first season together had been remarkable—and impossible to repeat.

"I know I'll never go through an experience like last season ever again," Webber said in the fall of 1992. "Not in my whole life. Not even if we stay together like one big, happy family and win it all the next three years. Last year was its own. Nothing that happened surprised me, but nothing will ever be the same as all that."

Others thought the Wolverines could do it again. The Associated Press put Michigan at the top of its pre-season rankings. Webber welcomed the challenge.

After playing two seasons for Michigan, Chris Webber announces his decision to enter the NBA draft.

"There is nothing we enjoy more than going into another team's gym with everybody screaming things at us, and coming out a win," he said.

Coach Fisher said he would have preferred to be ranked around No. 10 instead of first, but he thought his players could handle the No. 1 ranking.

As Michigan prepared to open the 1993 Big Ten season at Purdue on January 7, Webber said he planned to stay at Michigan for his junior season. The Wolverines won the game but the question of Webber jumping to the pros remained a continual distraction.

"Wherever I go," Webber said, "people always say something. They say, 'I know you're gonna go pro, Chris, but you should stay one more year.' Or they say: 'I know you're gonna stay, Chris, but you should go to the pros.'"

The *Detroit Free Press*'s Greg Stoda characterized Webber as "intelligent and reflective." Reporter Albom said, "Chris Webber, for all that muscle and bulk, for all those rim-hanging dunks . . . he is, and this may surprise you—as introspective and sensitive a college basketball player as you'll ever meet."

Coach Fisher shouts instructions to his Michigan Wolverines.

On January 12, 1993, second-ranked Michigan took on sixth-ranked Indiana at Crisler Arena. The Hoosiers, who would go on to win the Big Ten championship, blocked Webber's shot at the end of the game and won 76-75.

"I should have made the last play," Webber said. "It doesn't matter if four people were hanging on me."

A week later, Webber broke his nose in practice and needed surgery to repair it. He had also broken his nose while at Country Day.

He played in the next game wearing a mask to protect his nose. Michigan beat Minnesota in Minneapolis, 80-73.

On February 14, Michigan suffered another one-point loss at the hands of Indiana. Ironically, the Hoosiers star player, 6'7" Calbert Cheaney, would one day be Webber's pro teammate. Two weeks later, Michigan beat Ohio State, 66-64, the Wolverines' first win in Columbus since 1986.

As the 1992-93 season ended, Webber was voted to the AP All-America team, where he was joined by Cheaney and Duke's Bobby Hurley.

Webber started every one of his 70 games at Michigan. He averaged 17.4 points per game and made 59 percent of his field goal attempts. He averaged 10 rebounds and 2.5 blocks a game.

Michigan finished their schedule with a 26-4 record that gave them the top seed in the West Region for the 1993 NCAA tournament. Their first game would be against the West's 16th seed, the Coastal Carolina Chanticleers, a small school in Conway, South Carolina. The Wolverines swamped the Chanticleers, 84-53.

Two days later, facing UCLA before a crowd of 13,534 in Tucson, Michigan was ". . . standing on the cliff" as a sportswriter put it. "All their promise, their expectations, the entire weight of their own curious legend had suddenly come crashing down on them, knocking them to the floor."

Things looked grim when Michigan trailed 52-39 at the half, but in the second half they rediscovered Webber and Howard inside. The Wolverines gradually narrowed the UCLA lead and went ahead by eight with less than four minutes to play. However, two UCLA free throws with 6.3 seconds to play ended the game in regulation at 77-77.

It was still tied at 84 when Rose got the ball and put it up with 4.3 seconds to go. The ball

Chris Webber steals the ball from Purdue's Ian Stanbuck wearing a mask to protect a fractured nose.

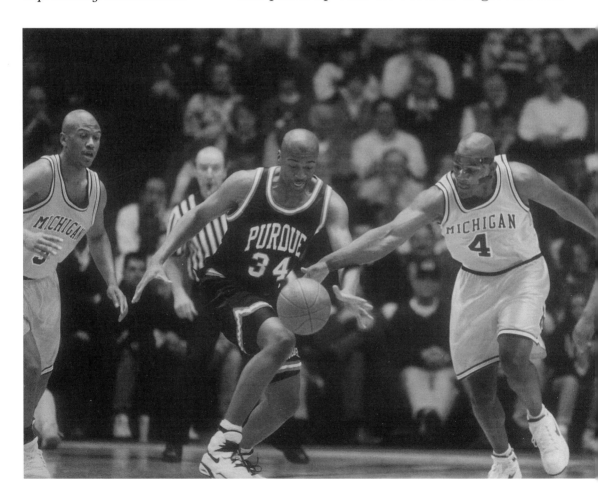

bounced off the rim, but King boarded off the weakside and scored the game winner with two seconds to play—final score: Michigan 86, UCLA 84. Webber led all scorers with 27 points along with a game-high 14 rebounds.

Next stop on the NCAA trail was Seattle, Washington. Michigan would play George Washington University of Washington, D.C., in the West Regional semifinals on March 26. The Colonels featured 7'1" freshman center Yinka Dare.

Michigan held Dare scoreless and won 72-64 to reach the regional finals on March 28. For the second year in a row, they would play Temple in an NCAA game. The Philadelphia school's veteran coach, John Chaney, had a strategy: "Don't let Chris Webber beat us." The Owls leaned on Webber throughout the game, but it didn't bring them a win. It was Michigan by 77-72.

For the second time in their two years at Michigan, the "Fab Five" were going to the Final Four.

Michigan's semifinal opponent in New Orleans on April 3 would be the Kentucky Wildcats. North Carolina would play Kansas in the other semifinal game.

The Wolverines won a place in a second straight NCAA title game with an 81-78 victory in overtime. North Carolina beat Kansas, 78-68.

So it was Michigan against North Carolina on April 5 for the championship. Michigan had won by one point, 79-78, when the teams had met three months earlier in the Rainbow Classic in Hawaii.

The North Carolina Tar Heels had one of college basketball's most successful coaches in Dean Smith, and they started Eric Montross, who had been heavily recruited by Michigan.

The Wolverines and Tar Heels battled throughout the game. Despite playing in the finals one year earlier, the five Michigan sophomores were nervous at the game's start as more than 64,000 fans watched in the Superdome. Michigan quickly trailed, but a rally capped by Webber's drive to the hoop gave the Wolverines a 15-9 lead. Converting a rebound, Webber was fouled and made the free throw to increase the lead. But North Carolina struggled back and led 42-36 at halftime.

The second half was a classic big-time college basketball battle. With the game tied at 56, Webber stuffed the ball off a lob from Howard. The lead continued to switch hands and with his team trailing 72-69, Webber captured a rebound and scored with only 36 seconds remaining to make it a one-point game. North Carolina's Pat Sullivan missed the second of a one-and-one free throw with 20 seconds to play.

Webber grabbed the rebound, dribbled the length of the court and in front of the Michigan bench he called for a time-out. "He screamed for it," said an observer at courtside.

But Michigan had used all its allotted time-outs. "The ref stared at [Webber] blankly," said the *Detroit Free Press*.

Because Webber had called a time-out when the team had none left, a technical foul was called against Michigan, giving North Carolina two free throws and the ball. The Tar Heels' Donald Williams made both free throws. The Tar Heels ran out the game, winning 76-71 to shatter the "Fab Five's" national title hopes a second time.

"It probably cost our team the game," Webber said afterwards. He repeated it again. And again. Coach Fisher said, "It cost us a chance. It didn't cost us the game."

Had the Michigan players been told in a time-out—their last legal one with 46 seconds left—that they had no more time-outs?

"It was stated," Jalen Rose said. But he added, "What's clear to somebody might not be clear to everybody."

"We thought we did . . .," Fisher said.

Said Webber, "I don't remember."

He noted the obvious: "If I knew we didn't have any time-outs left, then I wouldn't have called one."

Webber again was named to the Final Four All-Tournament team, becoming the first player in NCAA history to make the team as a freshman and a sophomore. But the ending of that championship game would be something he would never forget.

6

ON TO THE NBA

Despite his statement in January 1993 to the contrary, Webber decided to leave Michigan and announced on May 5, 1993, that he would enter the 1993 NBA draft on June 30.

He was expected to be the first pick in the draft, and the money was too much to pass up. When the Orlando Magic drafted Webber he was the first sophomore picked number one since 1979. That year a sophomore out of Michigan State named Earvin "Magic" Johnson was the first pick. Johnson would become one of the NBA's best players ever during his career with the Los Angeles Lakers.

Webber never played for Orlando, though. He was traded on draft day to the Golden State Warriors. Golden State sent guard Anfernee Hardaway and three future first round draft choices to Orlando in the trade.

In the fall of 1993, Webber began his NBA career. During his season in California, Webber

---

The NBA lured Webber away from college basketball. Here he plays in the NBA All-Star game in 1994.

47

Webber only dunked the ball for a short while for the Golden State Warriors before he was traded.

averaged 17.5 points for Golden State, second highest on the team, playing in 76 of 82 games. He averaged a team-high 9.1 rebounds a game and had a career-high 12 assists against the Los Angeles Clippers on December 23, 1993.

Webber became the first rookie in NBA history to total more than 1,000 points, 500 rebounds, 250 assists, 150 blocks, and 75 steals. He was the youngest player in Warriors history to lead the team in rebounds.

He was the Coca-Cola Classic NBA Rookie of the Year and was named to the 1994 NBA All-Rookies First Team by the league's head coaches.

During the 1994 NBA All-Star weekend in Minneapolis, he was the leading scorer with 18 and the leading rebounder with 10 in the first Schick Rookie Game.

Despite a fine season, Webber wasn't happy at Golden State. He and Warriors coach Don Nelson did not hit it off, and Webber was traded to the Washington Bullets on November 17, 1994, for Minnesota Timberwolves star Tom Gugliotta and three first-round draft choices.

The trade reunited two members of the "Fab Five" on the Bullets. (Washington would change its name to the Wizards before the 1997-98 season.) Webber's Michigan teammate Juwan Howard had been the Bullets first-round draft choice in 1994. Howard had been unsigned and reached a contract agreement on the day Webber was traded.

The Washington team also included former Big Ten foe Calbert Cheaney from Indiana who had been the Bullets first-round draft pick in 1993.

Washington, then coached by Jim Lynam, was

six games into the NBA season when they made the trade for Webber. He and Howard, who did not sign until the season had begun, made their first appearances in a 103-102 loss to the Boston Celtics at USAir Arena in suburban Landover, Maryland.

On December 22, 1994, Webber dislocated his left shoulder in a game at the Oakland Coliseum Arena against Golden State and missed 19 games. Late in the 1994-95 season, he had a career high 15 defensive rebounds against the Miami Heat. Playing in 54 games during the season, he increased his scoring average to a team-leading 20.1 points per game. He upped his rebounds per game to 9.6, and his 518 rebounds was tops on the Bullets.

Chris being guarded by Bill Curley of the Detroit Pistons.

He also led the team in field goal percentage, 49.5 percent, and steals—1.4 a game—but the Bullets had a woeful 21-61 record in 1994-95.

Shortly before the start of the 1995-96 season, Webber signed a six-year contract worth $58.5 million. Nine days later he reinjured his shoulder in a pre-season game, and four days later, in another exhibition game, he again dislocated the shoulder.

Webber returned to the lineup on November 30, 13 games into the season, but he played in only 15 games during the 1995-96 season. Still, his 23.7 points a game was the best on the team. Webber scored in double figures in every game he played.

Chicago Bull Michael Jordan shoots over Webber in the Bulls' quest for the 1997 NBA championship.

On December 27, 1995, he scored a career high 40 points against Golden State. He also had 10 rebounds and 10 assists for a triple-double. The Bullets won nine of the games Webber played, and Washington improved its season record to 39 wins and 43 losses.

After the season was over, Webber underwent surgery on the shoulder that had been giving him problems.

The 1996-97 season would see the Bullets make the playoffs, and Webber make his debut in the NBA All-Star Game in February 1997. A couple days later, Bickerstaff took over the Bullets coaching reins. He was president of the Denver Nuggets when he was chosen to replace Lynam, whom the team had fired when they were 22-25 at the All-Star break. Bickerstaff had been Bullets assistant coach from 1973 to 1985, including the Bullets' only NBA championship in 1978.

The Bullets' 1997 playoff run was short-lived. The newly-named Washington Wizards were swept in the first round by the Chicago Bulls, led by Michael Jordan. Washington lost a one-point game, 96-95, in the only home contest. Webber had 47 points in the three games. The Bulls would go on to win the NBA championship.

"REMARKABLE EFFORT" FALLS SHORT

On February 2, 1998, Webber strained his right shoulder in a game against Detroit and missed the next eight games of the 1997-98 season. When he came back against the Houston Rockets on February 24, he scored a season-best 36 points in a 124-112 Wizards victory.

On a Sunday afternoon toward the end of March, the Wizards were in East Rutherford, New Jersey, to play the Nets. New Jersey was then a game ahead of the Wizards in a fight for the final conference playoff spot. The Orlando Magic was also in the hunt.

The game in New Jersey was the first of a five-game road trip. The next four games would be on the West Coast and in Phoenix against four teams that were going to be in the playoffs.

During the third quarter of the game in East Rutherford, Washington seemed to be on the way to an important victory. But they blew an

As a Washington Wizard, Webber goes for the basket.

18-point lead, and the second half ended with the game tied 90-90.

It had not been a particularly good afternoon for Webber. He made only 10 of 24 field goal attempts. He missed five of his first eight free throws. Yet he was present at the end, even though he played the final two minutes and 42 seconds of overtime with five fouls, one short of being disqualified.

The Nets held a 98-96 lead with only 31.8 seconds to play in the overtime. Webber got the ball at the top of the key. He drove on Nets center Rony Seikaly and hooped a running layup to tie the game. He also drew a foul on Seikaly. He made the free throw for the lead and, after exchanging free throws, the Wizards had a 102-100 win.

The victory left the Wizards tied with the Orlando Magic for the eighth and final conference playoff position.

Webber said he wasn't planning on driving to the basket for what turned out to be the go-ahead shot. "Coach [Bernie Bickerstaff] drew up the play for me to set a back pick for Tracy [Murray] and then pop out for the ball. In the back of my mind, I was looking to drive and kick it out to one of our shooters. But I saw some daylight and took it."

Bickerstaff said after the game that he wasn't concerned about putting the ball in Webber's hands even though he had struggled for much of the game.

"It's what he gets paid to do," the coach said. "We gave him the ball and he made the play. If you give it to a guy in that situation, you have confidence in him."

The Wizards picked up only one more win on the road trip, losing three games in the next seven days. The victory came when they beat Portland, 99-77. They remained in the chase for the final playoff spot, a game behind the Orlando Magic and one-half game behind the Nets.

In mid-April 1998, however, things looked tough as the NBA season entered its final week. But Webber and his teammates met the challenge. Facing four games in five days, they won all of them.

On the final Tuesday of the season, the Wizards beat New York in Madison Square Garden, 104-102. Webber played 44 of the game's 48 minutes and scored 19 points. The next day, returning home to the MCI Center, Washington broke a four-game home losing streak. Webber had 14 points and a team-leading nine rebounds in 40 minutes in a 101-93 win over Cleveland.

Back on the road on Friday, the Wizards beat Miami 97-89. Webber had 21 points and 10 rebounds in 45 minutes. The Wizards' regular season ended on Saturday with another win at home against the Boston Celtics.

Three of the end-of-the-season wins were against playoff teams—New York, Cleveland, and Miami. While the Wizards were winning, New Jersey, which held the eighth playoff spot, lost three straight games.

The Wizards displayed "remarkable effort and concentration" during the winning streak, said the *Washington Post's* Ric Bucher.

But the effort was in vain. On the season's final day, the injury-riddled New Jersey Nets claimed the eighth and final Eastern Conference playoff berth. The Orlando Magic already had been eliminated from the playoff race, missing the playoffs for the first time in five years.

New Jersey made the playoffs by beating

Webber attempts to drive past the defense of Boston Celtic center Andrew DeClercq.

Detroit 114-101 in East Rutherford for their 43rd win of the season. The Nets won despite playing without two injured starters, point guard Sam Cassell and center Jayson William.

Wizards coach Bickerstaff said he was not going to watch the game on television. "But like an idiot, I did," he said. The Nets victory over the Pistons meant the Wizards season was over. They finished with a 42-40 mark, the 16th best record among the 29 NBA teams.

Webber led the Wizards in scoring and rebounding in the 1997-98 season. He averaged 21.9 points per game with a season high of 36 against the Houston Rockets on February 24. Webber pulled down an average of 9.5 rebounds a game, garnering 19 against the Charlotte Hornets on December 19. He also was only one of four NBA players with at least 100 steals—he had 111—and at least 100 blocks—he had 124.

Back in Washington, rumors of Chris Webber being traded had been circulating for weeks. On the day the 1997-98 season ended, Washington general manager Wes Unseld, once a star center in the NBA, said he was going to wait to assess the just-ended season.

"But I think everybody, of course, is disappointed," Unseld said. "I'm not going to get into any of my plans because I haven't made any."

Unseld said he was going "to have to take into consideration injuries and key players being out" and then make some recommendations.

On May 14, 1998, rumor became fact. The Wizards traded Webber to the Sacamento Kings in exchange for two veteran players, Mitch Richmond and Otis Thorpe.

"We gave up a tremendous young talent in Chris Webber," said Unseld. "Webber has done a lot for this team."

Unseld also addressed the criticism that Washington was hurt by starting two players—Webber and Howard—who were both power forwards. "We had two very, very talented young men playing basically the same position," he said.

"In Chris Webber we have acquired one of the NBA's impact players, and he is only 25 years old," said Sacramento vice president of basketball operations Geoff Petrie. He said it was difficult to trade a player of Richmond's ability, "but with Chris we acquire a younger player we can build our team around."

Petrie said the Kings "certainly needed more size and more skill on our front line. Chris Webber possesses a lot of those qualities.

"He ranks in a very elite group of players in

Webber reaches over Houston Rocket guard Brent Price in a game in which he scored 36 points.

the league," Petrie said. "He has been a force since he came into the league. . . . He has all the tools to be an All-Star for many years to come."

The trade came eight days after Webber told the *Washington Post* that he wanted to stay with the Wizards. Webber "sounded like a changed man," wrote Ric Bucher.

"I don't want to make the same mistakes anymore and that's why I want to come back," Webber had told the *Post.* He said he "used to fight unwinnable battles and I don't plan to do that anymore.

"I'm so at peace right now, even with everything that is going on." Webber was speaking of the fact that he was facing criminal charges stemming from a traffic stop in Prince George's County, Maryland, earlier in the year. He was stopped for speeding during the early morning hours of January 20. The traffic stop led to charges of second-degree assault and possession of marijuana and six traffic violations. On May 11, Webber lost his driving privileges in Maryland for 120 days for refusing to take a blood test after the January traffic stop.

The day after Webber's interview with Bucher, Webber's attorney requested and was granted a jury trial on the charges. Both Webber's attorney and the Prince George's County state's attorney's office said they hoped to reach a plea agreement before trial.

Despite his troubles, Webber said he wanted to be in Washington. "But wherever I am next year, we're going to make some noise, I can promise you that."

"Webber," wrote *Washington Post* reporter Michael Wilbon in 1998, "is as smart and as engaging and charismatic a young man as you could hope to have on your team. You meet Webber's family, and you know there wasn't a lot of foolishness tolerated around his home. The talent's there, it's the commitment a lot of us wonder about."

Webber, now 25, will go to camp in the fall of 1998 to prepare for his sixth NBA season as a member of the Sacramento Kings.

The *San Francisco Chronicle's* David Steele wrote, "There is so much he hasn't achieved. A playoff victory for one thing. . . . Or the presence of mind and body to lead, rather than follow."

Five years earlier, "The NBA made it clear [Webber] was the cream of the 1993 crop," Steele said. "Whoever took him was going to lift its team upon his shoulders and ask him to start hauling.

"Maybe one player per generation can handle that. Webber was not the one for this generation."

Perhaps the expectations for Webber were a hindrance. The question remains if he can pull up an entire NBA team as he had done in high school and college. Then, his promise will have been fulfilled.

"Chris Webber can do it all," said Sacramento coach Eddie Jordan. "He is one of the most dynamic players in the game today. Our staff can't wait to begin working with him."

Webber warms up for a game the day after he was arrested for possession of marijuana.

CHRONOLOGY

1973   Born March 1, 1973, in Detroit, Michigan

1989   Leads Birmingham Detroit Country Day High School as a sophomore to the 1989 Michigan Class C state championship, where they win

1990   Country Day High School moves up a class and wins Class B championship with Webber scoring 30 points

1991   As a senior is National High School Player of the Year; named Mr. Basketball in Michigan; recruited by the University of Michigan; arrives on Michigan campus with three other highly sought high school players

1992   Starts with four other freshman for Michigan in NCAA finals; they lose game to Duke, 71-51

1993   Named to the Final Four All-Tournament team, becoming the first player in NCAA history to make the team as a freshman and a sophomore; drafted by the Orlando Magic with the first pick in the 1993 NBA draft, making him the first college sophomore picked No. 1 since 1979; traded the same day to the Golden State Warriors

1994   Wins the 1994 Coca-Cola Classic NBA Rookie of the Year Award; named to the 1994 NBA All-Rookies First Team by the league's head coaches; traded to the Washington Bullets in November; is injured in December and misses next 19 games

1995   Signs six-year $58.5 million contract; undergoes surgery on shoulder in off-season

1997   Makes NBA All-Star team

1998   Traded on May 14 to the Sacamento Kings in exchange for two veteran players, Mitch Richmond and Otis Thorpe

STATISTICS

CHRIS WEBBER

NBA Statistics

Year	G	FGM	FGA	PTS	PPG	RBG	BLK	AST	APG	STL
1993-94	76	572	1,037	1,333	17.5	9.1	164	272	3.6	93
1994-95	54	464	938	1,085	20.1	9.6	85	256	4.7	83
1995-96	15	150	276	356	23.7	7.6	9	75	5.0	27
1996-97	72	604	1,167	1,445	20.1	10.3	137	331	4.6	122
1997-98	71	647	1,346	1,555	21.9	9.5	124	273	3.8	111
Career	288	2,437	4,759	5,774	20.0	9.5	519	1,207	4.2	436

G	games
FGM	field goals made
FGA	field goals attempted
PTS	points
PPG	points per game
RPG	rebounds per game
BLK	blocks
AST	assists
APG	assists per game
STL	steals

FURTHER READING

Albom, Mitch. "Stalking Chris Webber: Fame Brings Bids, but Precious Little Time To Be a Kid." *Detroit Free Press*, February 28, 1991.

Bucher, Ric. "Changed Webber Wants to Stay in D.C." *Washington Post*, May 7, 1998.

Sirak, Ron. *Juwan Howard*. Philadelphia: Chelsea House Publishers, 1998.

Steele, David. "His Show Comes to Sacramento." *San Francisco Chronicle*, May 15, 1998.

Stoda, Greg. "5 Easy Pieces, Wolverines; Fab Sophomores Coolly Set Course to NCAA Title." *Detroit Free Press*, December 1, 1992.

Tuttle, Dennis. *The Composite Guide to Basketball*. Philadelphia: Chelsea House Publishers, 1998.

ABOUT THE AUTHOR

Paul J. Deegan has written some 80 juvenile books including titles on the United States Supreme Court, American universities, and the nations of the Persian Gulf. Subjects of the many biographies he's written include presidents and athletes.

Paul is a graduate of the University of Minnesota. A former newspaper editor, he has worked for years in juvenile publishing as an editor and administrator.

Paul and his wife, Dorothy, have three adult children and five grandchildren. They reside in Eden Prairie, Minnesota, a suburb of Minneapolis.

oto Credits
*/Wide World Photos: pp. 2, 8, 10, 12, 17, 19, 20, 22, 26, 30, 32, 35, 37, 38, 40, 42, 46, 48, 49, 50, 52, , 57, 59; Detroit Free Press: p. 14.

INDEX

Albom, Mitch, 19, 24, 40

Bickerstaff, Bernie, 10, 11, 51, 54, 56

Boston Celtics, 49, 55

Bucher, Ric, 55, 58

Cassell, Sam, 56

Chaney, John, 43

Charlotte Hornets, 56

Cheaney, Calbert, 41, 48

Chicago Bulls, 51

Cincinnati Bearcats, 36

Cleveland Cavaliers, 9-13

Coastal Carolina University (Chanticleers), 41

Country Day High School (Yellowjackets), 18-21, 23-27

Dapper Dan Roundball Classic, 28

Dare, Yinka, 43

Detroit Mercy, 32

Detroit Pistons, 56

Detroit Superfriends, 21, 29

Duke University (Blue Devils), 36, 37

"Fab Five," 25, 28, 29, 34, 35, 37, 39-45, 48

Fife, Dugan, 29

Fisher, Steve, 31, 33, 40, 44, 45

Frey, Jennifer, 13

George Washington University, 43

Golden State Warriors, 47-48, 49, 51

Gugliotta, Tom, 48

Hardaway, Anfernee, 47

Heathcote, Jeff, 16

Hill, Grant, 37

Houston Rockets, 53, 56

Howard, Juwan, 9, 11, 12, 13, 25, 28, 29, 31, 33, 34, 35, 42, 48, 49, 57

Hurley, Bobby, 37, 41

Indiana University (Hoosiers), 34-35, 36, 40-41

Inkster Temple Christian School, 16, 18

Ishpeming High School, 20

Jackson, Ray, 28, 31, 33, 34, 35

Johnson, Earvin "Magic," 47

Jordan, Eddie, 59

Jordan, Michael, 51

Keener, Kurt, 18, 21, 23

King, Jimmy, 25, 31, 33, 34, 35, 43

Knight, Bobby, 24

Krzyzewski, Mike, 37

Laettner, Christian, 37

Lenard, Voshon, 28

Los Angeles Lakers, 47

Lynam, Jim, 48, 51

MacLeod, John, 34

Majerle, Dan, 9

McDonald's All-American Game, 28

Miami Heat, 49, 55

Michigan State University, 16

Montross, Eric, 32, 43

Muresan, Gheorghe, 13

Murray, Tracy, 54

NCAA tournament, 1992, 35

NCAA tournament, 1993, 41-45

Nelson, Don, 48

New Jersey Nets, 53-54, 55-56

New York Knicks, 55

North Carolina University (Tar Heels), 43-44

Notre Dame University, 33-34

Ohio State University, 35, 41

Oklahoma State University, 35

Orlando Magic, 47, 53, 54, 55

Petrie, Geoff, 57-58

Richmond, Mitch, 57

Rose, Jalen, 28, 29, 31, 33, 34, 35, 36, 42, 45

Sacramento Kings, 57, 59

Saganaw Buena Vista High School, 21

Seikaly, Rony, 54

Smith, Dean, 43

Steele, David, 59

Stoda, Greg, 36, 40

Strickland, Rod, 11

Sullivan, Pat, 44

Talley, Mike, 33, 37

Temple University, 35, 43

Thorpe, Otis, 57

UCLA, 41-43

Unseld, Wes, 57

University of Kentucky (Wildcats), 35, 43

University of Michigan (Wolverines), 24, 25, 27, 28, 29, 31-37, 39-45, 47

Washington Bullets/Wizards, 9-13, 48, 51, 53-56, 57

Webber, Chris

childhood, 15-21

college decision, 24-28

college years, 31-45, 47

with Golden State Warriors, 47-48

high school years, 23-28

honors, 20, 26, 27, 28, 41, 45, 48

injuries, 41, 49, 50, 53

legal problems, 58-59

in 1993 NBA draft, 47

statistics, 48, 49, 50, 51, 56-57

with Washington Bullets/Wizards, 48-59

Webber, Doris, 15, 16, 27

Webber, Mayce, 15, 16-17

Wilbon, Michael, 58

William, Jayson, 56